WHAT I KNOW ABOUT

NATURE

Gibbs Smith

First Edition
29 28 27 26 25   5 4 3 2 1

Compilation © 2025 Gibbs Smith

Published by
Gibbs Smith
570 N. Sportsplex Dr.
Kaysville, Utah 84037

1.800.835.4993 orders
www.gibbs-smith.com

Designed by Sheryl Dickert
Printed and bound in China

This product is made of FSC®-certified and other controlled material.

Library of Congress Control Number: 2024941769

ISBN: 978-1-4236-6841-1

INTRODUCTION

Nature is what we, as earth's inhabitants, have in common. We all breathe the same air, drink the same water. At night, we gaze upon the same dome of stars. We delight at a flower in bloom, marvel at the change of seasons, are humbled by the power of ocean waves. We're fascinated by the fragility of a butterfly's wings.

What I Know About Nature celebrates our sense of wonder and gently reminds us to care for our natural world by presenting 125 quotes from some of the best minds throughout history.

John Muir, Theodore Roosevelt, Rachel Carson, Edward Abbey, and Jane Goodall, among others, share insights on the beauty of nature and the human experience of the outdoors and wilderness.

This book reminds us that nature is our home. We are invited to delight in it and called upon to care for it.

A morning-glory at my window satisfies

me more than the metaphysics of books.

—WALT WHITMAN

The air is like a butterfly

With frail blue wings.

The happy earth looks at the sky

And sings.

—JOYCE KILMER

I felt my lungs inflate with the onrush of scenery—

air, mountains, trees, people. I thought,

"This is what it is to be happy."

—SYLVIA PLATH

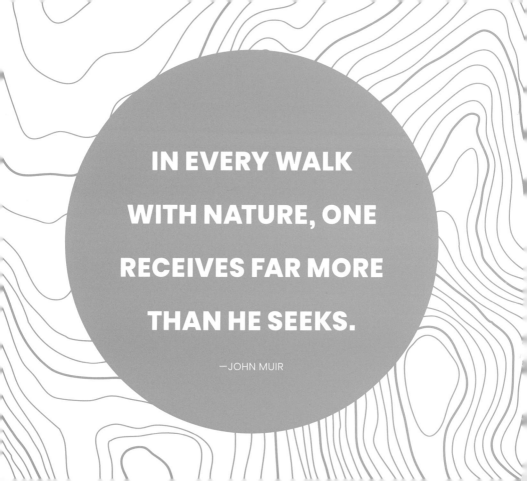

IN EVERY WALK WITH NATURE, ONE RECEIVES FAR MORE THAN HE SEEKS.

—JOHN MUIR

While my interest in natural history has added very little to my sum of achievement, it has added immeasurably to my sum of enjoyment in life.

—THEODORE ROOSEVELT

The human spirit needs places where nature has not been rearranged by the hand of man.

—UNKNOWN

A walk in nature walks the soul back home.

—MARY DAVIS

Adopt the pace of nature: her secret is patience.

—RALPH WALDO EMERSON

The more high-tech we become, the more nature we need.

—RICHARD LOUV

The best remedy for those who are

afraid, lonely, or unhappy is to go outside,

somewhere where they can be quiet, alone

with the heavens, nature, and God.

—ANNE FRANK

Always be on the lookout

for the presence of wonder.

—E. B. WHITE

Time in nature is not leisure time; it's an

essential investment in our children's health

(and also, by the way, in our own).

—RICHARD LOUV

Climb the mountains and get their good tidings. Nature's peace will flow into you as sunshine flows into trees. The winds will blow their own freshness into you, and the storms their energy, while cares will drop away from you like the leaves of autumn.

—JOHN MUIR

When anxious, uneasy, and bad thoughts come,

I go to the sea, and the sea drowns them out

with its great wide sounds, cleanses me with its

noise, and imposes a rhythm upon everything in

me that is bewildered and confused.

—RAINER MARIA RILKE

Come forth into the

light of things, let nature

be your teacher.

—WILLIAM WORDSWORTH

Human subtlety will never devise an invention more beautiful, more simple, or more direct than does nature, because in her inventions nothing is lacking and nothing is superfluous.

—LEONARDO DA VINCI

In nature, nothing is
perfect and everything
is perfect. Trees can
be contorted, bent
in weird ways, and
they're still beautiful.

—ALICE WALKER

Nature indifferently copied is far superior to the best idealities.

—JOHN JAMES AUDUBON

Keep your love of nature, for that

is the true way to understand

art more and more.

—VINCENT VAN GOGH

Nature is the art of God.

—DANTE ALIGHIERI

The silence of nature is very real.

It surrounds you, you can feel it.

—TED TRUEBLOOD

Look deep into nature, and then you will understand everything better.

—ALBERT EINSTEIN

At sunrise, the blue sky paints herself with

gold colors and joyfully dances to the

music of a morning breeze.

—DEBASISH MRIDHA

Eternal sunrise, eternal sunset,

eternal dawn and gloaming, on seas

and continents and islands, each in

its turn, as the round earth rolls.

—JOHN MUIR

Spring afternoon, beautiful flowery meadow, gentle breeze touching the heart, this is the magic of life.

—DEBASISH MRIDHA

The mountains are calling and I must go.

—JOHN MUIR

The mountains, I become a part of it . . .

The herbs, the fir tree, I become a part of it.

The morning mists, the clouds, the gathering waters,

I become a part of it.

The wilderness, the dew drops, the pollen . . .

I become a part of it.

—NAVAJO CHANT

Nature is a mutable cloud which

is always and never the same.

—RALPH WALDO EMERSON

The sound of the rain needs no translation.

—ALAN WATTS

I hear the wind among the trees

Playing the celestial symphonies;

I see the branches downward bent,

Like keys of some great instrument.

—HENRY WADSWORTH LONGFELLOW

Every leaf speaks bliss to me,

Fluttering from the autumn tree.

—EMILY BRONTE

I never saw a discontented tree.

They grip the ground as though they

liked it, and though fast rooted they

travel about as far as we do.

—JOHN MUIR

Trees are the earth's

endless effort to speak to

the listening heaven.

—RABINDRANATH TAGORE

There is pleasure in the pathless woods,

There is rapture in the lonely shore,

There is society where none intrudes,

By the deep Sea, and music in its roar:

I love not Man the less, but Nature more.

—LORD BYRON

The sea is everything.

It covers seven tenths of the terrestrial globe. Its breath is pure and healthy. It is an immense desert, where man is never lonely, for he feels life stirring on all sides.

—JULES VERNE

The ocean is

everything I

want to be.

Beautiful,

mysterious, wild,

and free.

—UNKNOWN

The sea, once it casts its spell, holds

one in its net of wonder forever.

—JACQUES YVES COUSTEAU

The ocean stirs the heart, inspires the imagination,

and brings eternal joy to the soul.

—ROBERT WYLAND

The river moves,

but it follows

a path. When it

tires of one journey,

it rubs through some rock

to forge a new way.

Hard work, but that's

its nature.

—KEKLA MAGOON

The finest workers of stone are not copper or steel tools, but the gentle touches of air and water working at their leisure with a liberal allowance of time.

—HENRY DAVID THOREAU

Rivers are roads which move, and which

carry us whither we desire to go.

BLAISE PASCAL

A river seems a magic thing.

A magic, moving, living part of

the very earth itself.

—LAURA GILPIN

Rivers know this: there is no hurry.

We shall get there someday.

—A. A. MILNE

Flowers are the sweetest things God ever made and forgot to put a soul into.

—HENRY WARD BEECHER

THE EARTH LAUGHS IN FLOWERS.

—RALPH WALDO EMERSON

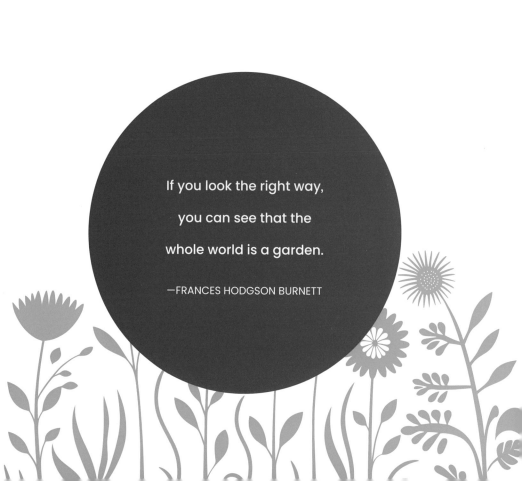

If you look the right way,

you can see that the

whole world is a garden.

—FRANCES HODGSON BURNETT

Every flower is a soul blossoming in nature.

—GÉRARD DE NERVAL

The bluebird carries

the sky on his back.

-HENRY DAVID THOREAU

The butterfly counts not months but

moments, and has time enough.

—RABINDRANATH TAGORE

Animals are such agreeable friends—they ask no questions; they pass no criticisms.

—GEORGE ELIOT

The animal shall not be measured
by man. In a world older and more
complete than ours, they move finished
and complete, gifted with extensions of
the senses we have lost or never attained,
living by voices we shall never hear.

—HENRY BESTON

The love for all living creatures is

the most noble attribute of man.

—CHARLES DARWIN

Nature gives to every time and season some beauties of its own.

—CHARLES DICKENS

Sunshine is delicious, rain is refreshing,

wind braces us up, snow is exhilarating;

there is really no such thing as bad weather,

only different kinds of good weather.

—JOHN RUSKIN

The seasons are what a symphony ought to be:

four perfect movements in harmony with each other.

—ARTHUR RUBINSTEIN

In the spring, at

the end of the

day, you should

smell like dirt.

—MARGARET ATWOOD

Summer afternoon—

summer afternoon;

to me those have always

been the two most

beautiful words in the

English language.

—HENRY JAMES

In summer,

the song sings itself.

—WILLIAM CARLOS WILLIAMS

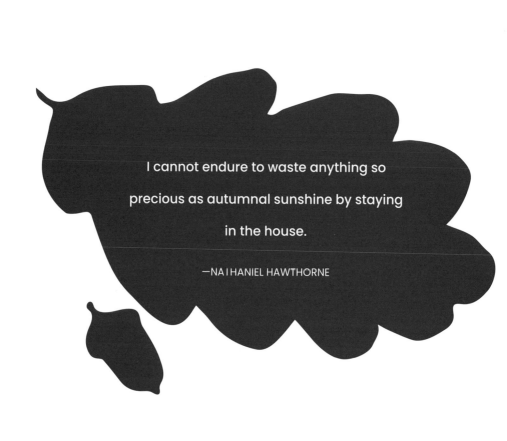

I cannot endure to waste anything so precious as autumnal sunshine by staying in the house.

—NATHANIEL HAWTHORNE

Autumn is a second spring when every leaf is a flower.

—ALBERT CAMUS

Life starts all over again when it gets crisp in the fall.

—F. SCOTT FITZGERALD

I'm so glad I live in a world

where there are Octobers.

—L. M. MONTGOMERY

Autumn . . .

the year's last, loveliest smile.

—WILLIAM CULLEN BRYANT

One must maintain a little bit of summer, even in the middle of winter.

—HENRY DAVID THOREAU

To appreciate the beauty of

a snowflake it is necessary to

stand out in the cold.

—ATTRIBUTED TO ARISTOTLE

There is something infinitely healing in the

repeated refrains of nature—the assurance that

dawn comes after night, and spring after winter.

—RACHEL CARSON

The sky and the sun are always there.

It's the clouds that come and go.

—RACHEL JOYCE

EVERY SUNSET BRINGS THE PROMISE OF A NEW DAWN.

—RALPH WALDO EMERSON

The sun, with all those planets revolving around it and dependent on it, can still ripen a bunch of grapes as if it had nothing else in the universe to do.

—GALILEO GALILEI

The sky is filled with stars,

invisible by day.

—HENRY WADSWORTH LONGFELLOW

The stars are the jewels of the night, and perchance

surpass anything which day has to show.

–HENRY DAVID THOREAU

The moon doth with delight

Look round her when the

heavens are bare,

Waters on a starry night

Are beautiful and fair.

—WILLIAM WORDSWORTH

The stars are the landmarks of the universe.

—JOHN HERSCHEL

The stars are forth, the moon above the tops

Of the snow-shining mountains. —Beautiful!

I linger yet with Nature, for the night

Hath been to me a more familiar face

Than that of man.

—LORD BYRON

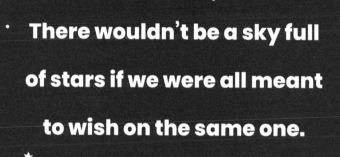

There wouldn't be a sky full of stars if we were all meant to wish on the same one.

—FRANCES CLARK

Keep your eyes on the stars,

and your feet on the ground.

—THEODORE ROOSEVELT

The cosmos is within us. We are made of star-stuff.

We are a way for the universe to know itself.

—CARL SAGAN

The clearest way into the Universe is through a forest wilderness.

—JOHN MUIR

The farther one gets into the wilderness, the greater is the attraction of its lonely freedom.

—THEODORE ROOSEVELT

To sit in solitude, to think in solitude with only the music of the stream and the cedar to break the flow of silence, there lies the value of wilderness.

—JOHN MUIR

Wilderness is not a luxury but a necessity of the human spirit, and as vital to our lives as water and good bread.

—EDWARD ABBEY

Heaven is under our feet

as well as over our heads.

—HENRY DAVID THOREAU

I believe that there is a subtle magnetism in nature,

which, if we unconsciously yield to it, will direct us aright.

—HENRY DAVID THOREAU

For a time, I rest in the grace of the

world, and am free.

—WENDELL BERRY

In all things of nature there is

something of the marvelous.

—ARISTOTLE

The richness I achieve comes from nature, the source of my inspiration.

—CLAUDE MONET

Those who contemplate the beauty

of the earth find reserves of strength

that will endure as long as life lasts.

—RACHEL CARSON

A grove of giant redwood or sequoias

should be kept just as we keep a great

and beautiful cathedral.

—THEODORE ROOSEVELT

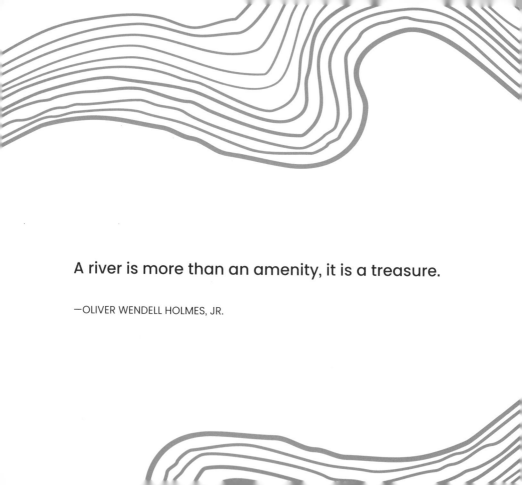

A river is more than an amenity, it is a treasure.

—OLIVER WENDELL HOLMES, JR.

If we save our wild places, we will ultimately save ourselves.

—STEVE IRWIN

The earth does not belong to us;

we belong to the earth.

—CHIEF SEATTLE

A true conservationist is a man who knows that the world is not given by his fathers, but borrowed from his children.

—JOHN JAMES AUDUBON

We must protect the forests for our children, grandchildren, and children yet to be born. We must protect the forests for those who can't speak for themselves such as the birds, animals, fish, and trees.

—HEREDITARY CHIEF QWATSINAS (EDWARD MOODY), NUXALK NATION

Some may wonder why I chose wildflowers when there are hunger and unemployment and the big bomb in the world. Well, I, for one, think we will survive, and I hope that along the way we can keep alive our experience with the flowering earth. For the bounty of nature is also one of the deep needs of man.

—LADY BIRD JOHNSON

The wild things of this earth are not ours to do with as we please. They have been given to us in trust, and we must account for them to the generation which will come after us, and audit our accounts.

—WILLIAM T. HORNADAY

Surely, we do not want to live in a world without the great apes. . . . A world not enhanced by the sight of a grizzly bear and her cubs hunting for berries in the wilderness? What would our grandchildren think if these magical images were only to be found in books?

—JANE GOODALL

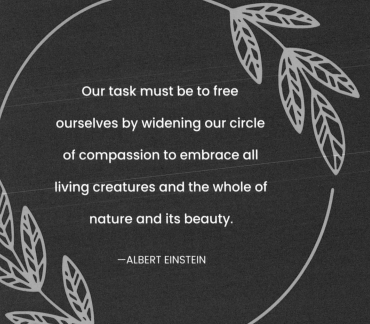

Our task must be to free
ourselves by widening our circle
of compassion to embrace all
living creatures and the whole of
nature and its beauty.

—ALBERT EINSTEIN

The wildlife and its habitat cannot speak, so we must and we will.

—THEODORE ROOSEVELT

The environment is where

we all meet; where we all have

a mutual interest; it is the one

thing all of us share.

—LADY BIRD JOHNSON

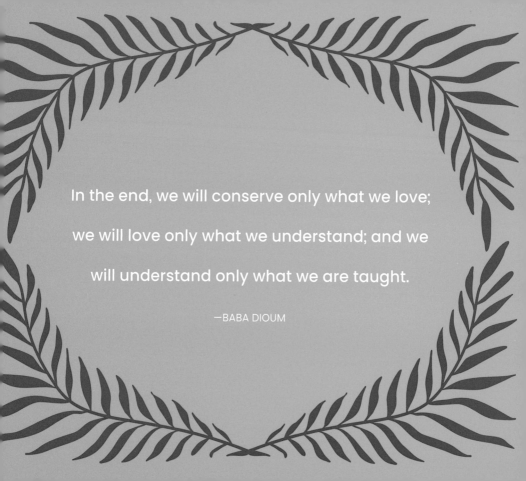

In the end, we will conserve only what we love;

we will love only what we understand; and we

will understand only what we are taught.

—BABA DIOUM

We can move toward a world where we live in harmony with nature. Where we live in harmony with each other. No matter what nation we come from. No matter what our religion. No matter what our culture.

—JANE GOODALL

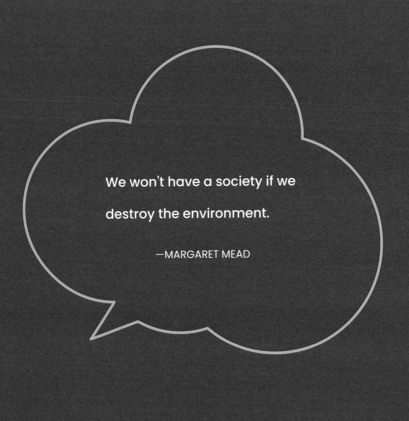

The greatest threat to our planet is the

belief that someone else will save it.

—ROBERT SWAN

To forget how to dig the

earth and to tend the soil is

to forget ourselves.

—MAHATMA GANDHI

We cannot protect something we do not love, we cannot love what we do not know, and we cannot know what we do not see. Or hear. Or sense.

—RICHARD LOUV

To lose the chance to see frigate birds soaring in circles above the storm, or a file of pelicans winging their way homeward across the crimson afterglow of the sunset, or a myriad of terns flashing in the bright light of midday as they hover in a shifting maze above the beach—why, the loss is like the loss of a gallery of the masterpieces of the artists of old time.

—THEODORE ROOSEVELT

The more clearly we can focus our

attention on the wonders and realities

of the universe about us, the less

taste we shall have for destruction.

—RACHEL CARSON

Man did not weave the web of life, he

is merely a strand in it. Whatever he

does to the web, he does to himself.

—CHIEF SEATTLE

We still do not know one thousandth of one

percent of what nature has revealed to us.

—ALBERT EINSTEIN

The care of the earth is our most ancient and

most worthy, and after all our most pleasing

responsibility. To cherish what remains of it and

to foster its renewal is our only hope.

—WENDELL BERRY

Destroying rainforest for economic gain is like

burning a Renaissance painting to cook a meal.

—E. O. WILSON

The air is precious ...

for all things share the same breath—the beast,

the tree, the man, they all share the same breath.

—CHIEF SEATTLE

The earth is what we all have in common.

—WENDELL BERRY

Nature is loved by what is best in us.

—RALPH WALDO EMERSON

Nature is orderly.

That which appears to be chaotic in nature

is only a more complex kind of order.

—GARY SNYDER

NATURE DOES NOT HURRY, YET EVERYTHING IS ACCOMPLISHED.

—LAO TZU

To see a world in a grain of sand

and heaven in a wildflower

hold infinity in the palm of your hand,

and eternity in an hour.

—WILLIAM BLAKE

Nature is pleased with simplicity.

—ISAAC NEWTON

The goal of life is to make your heartbeat match the

beat of the universe, to match your nature with nature.

—JOSEPH CAMPBELL

I remember every stone, every tree,

the scent of heather . . . Even when the

thunder growled in the distance, and the

wind swept up the valley in fitful gusts,

oh, it was beautiful, home sweet home.

—BEATRIX POTTER

Nature is not
a place to visit.
It is home.

—GARY SNYDER

Now I see the secret of making the best persons,

it is to grow in the open air and to eat and sleep

with the earth.

—WALT WHITMAN

May your trails be crooked, winding, lonesome, dangerous,

leading to the most amazing view. May your mountains rise

into and above the clouds. May your rivers flow without end.

—EDWARD ABBEY

Study nature,

love nature,

stay close to nature.

It will never fail you.

—FRANK LLOYD WRIGHT

I believe the world is incomprehensibly beautiful—

an endless prospect of magic and wonder.

—ANSEL ADAMS